Procrastination

Proven Tactics To Master Your Time, Supercharge Productivity And Conquer Your Inner Procrastinator Once And For All

By Adam Richards

Table of Contents

Introduction

What This Book Is About

In the first chapter you will learn all about procrastination, when it can be classified as procrastinating and when not, and the 3 basic categories of people with procrastinating tendencies. You will then be able to determine for yourself whether you are a procrastinator or not.

In the second chapter, we will go into the 10 common warning signs that indicate someone is a chronic procrastinator. Such warning signs are avoidance and lack of commitment, perfectionism, fear of failure or success etc.

In the next chapter you will learn more than 10 different ways that if you implement in your life, will definitely help you gradually overcome procrastination. Some of these ways are for example, starting easy and slowly, not overthinking things, learning to start anywhere and taking action.

In the fourth chapter you will find information about goal setting using the S.M.A.R.T. method. If you haven't heard of the term before here is what it stands for:

Specific

Measurable

Attainable

Realistic

Timely

It is without a doubt one of the best ways to set goals, as it will dramatically increase your chances of achieving them.

In the fifth chapter you will learn about the classic, yet extremely effective when used properly Pareto Principle (also known as 80/20 rule). You will learn where you should focus on, how to prioritize and how to increase your daily productivity.

Finally, in the last chapter you will be given information on 8 powerful habits, that should you include in your day-to-day life, can dramatically increase your chances of overcoming procrastination for good.

After all procrastination is merely a habit and you can simply replace it with a new healthier and more productive one. You will learn how to focus on the now, why you should be using a task manager or day planner, eliminating distractions etc.

Once again, thank you for purchasing this book, I hope you enjoy it!

Chapter 1:
What Everyone Ought To Know About Procrastination

"I will do it later" / "I work better under deadline pressure"

These are all things that each one of us has done at one point in life. Procrastination is the behavior of opting to do other pleasurable or less important activities instead of important ones. It involves pushing tasks to a later date, pushing them close to the deadline or simply putting off such stressing or strenuous tasks for later.

In other instances, some of these activities don't necessarily have to be strenuous. For instance, you could opt not to make a call to your customers today because you feel that now is not a good time. You could also postpone; going to college, cleaning your plate after a meal etc. People can postpone literally anything in life including getting married, getting kids etc.

Procrastination can be classified by these three behavioral criteria. It is:

1. Counter productive
2. Needless
3. Delaying.

Putting a task off does not necessarily mean you are procrastinating; it only counts as procrastination if there is no adequate reason for putting off the task at hand. Procrastination to some degree is normal. However, when the procrastination impedes normal activity, then it is considered chronic procrastination. This is the surest "one way ticket" to failure in life since it effectively puts perceived difficulties and mountains on the highway to success.

Why would anyone do that to themselves?

Most procrastinators when asked why they do it said it was more of a lifestyle, a sort of mechanism that they use to justify their chronic procrastination or inability to get things done promptly. Research has indicated that 20% of all American adults are chronic procrastinators; this number is higher than all the diagnosed cases of chronic depression.

As earlier stated, almost everyone procrastinates but not everyone is a chronic procrastinator. Procrastination could be the reason why you always file your income tax returns late, or delay waking up in the morning when you know very well that you are going to be in a hectic rush to complete your morning rituals when you are pressed for time. In most cases, we do not realize that our normal procrastination has turned chronic until it is too late. In reality, chronic procrastination can have severe adverse effects on your life.

We shall discuss some not so fun, yet interesting facts about procrastination that will probably open your eyes and get you to start doing something about this habit, if you find yourself behaving this way.

All about procrastination

Most people delude themselves into thinking that procrastination is a time management problem, which in fact is not the case. Procrastinators are aware of the time and can effectively manage it; they just choose not to. To be honest, every time you hit the 5 minute snooze button and go back to sleep, knowing very well that you will get stuck in traffic and lie to your boss or supervisor that your car failed to start, does not mean that you are not aware of time; you are aware of time and have planned for it. The truth is; you are just choosing not to follow the time plan that you have set out.

This alleged time mismanagement cuts across all circles of your life if you are a chronic procrastinator. You may find that even though you are aware of the income tax returns deadline, you wait for the last minute rush to do it, which as you already know brings with it immense levels of stress and anxiety.

Procrastination is not a disease, at least not in the traditional sense of the word. Although, no one is born a procrastinator, researchers have found a positive relationship between authoritarian family settings and the development of this habit. In such family settings, children fail to develop self-regulating skills, which means they are likely to start procrastinating as a form of rebellion.

Another interesting thing about procrastinators is that they are perennial liars, to themselves. As you already know, if you are a procrastinator, you have countless reasons as to why you cannot do the tasks you are supposed to do when they should be done.

Let's be honest, you could have done many of the tasks that you are trying to justify why you didn't do. If you are the type that is always telling yourself that you will do a task in the next hour, in the next few hours, tomorrow or next week, you are in a dangerous cycle. Don't lie to yourself that you work well under pressure; what's the point of not sleeping for an entire week during the examinations week when you could have read comfortably throughout the semester?

Even though we procrastinate for different reasons, procrastination can be divided into three basic categories:

Arousal types

These are those people who get a thrill out of the last minute rush, that comes out of waiting until the last minute and then rushing to accomplish certain tasks. If you are this kind of person, you can be described as a thrill seeker procrastinator because you tend to get a euphoric rush out of procrastination and waiting for the last minute.

Avoider types

Some people simply have a tendency of putting off doing something due to fear of failure or success. If you have this kind of procrastination, you probably are the kind who is overly concerned about what other people think of you and would rather have people thinking that you didn't have time to do something as opposed to thinking that you are incompetent.

Decisional procrastinators

This division of procrastinators cannot make a decision even if their life depended on it. Even when they are confronted with a logical choice between two conflicting decisions, they will find a way to make excuses. They do this so that they can absolve themselves from any eventuality or responsibility that may accompany the decision that they make.

Think of how you procrastinate. If you are the kind who simply doesn't like taking responsibility and would rather pass on making important or life changing decisions, you most likely fall in this category.

I know how hard it is not to say that you are going to do something at some other time simply because you don't feel like doing it (you lack any valid reason why you have to do it later). Actually, many are the times when we procrastinate without even thinking that we are doing it; procrastination has become so much part of us such that it is like coughing, sneezing or farting. You don't really give too much thought into it when you do it.

However, when it starts affecting your productivity, it is paramount that you do something now. You may wonder whether it is practically possible to put an end to procrastination despite it becoming highly engrained in us. Before we can discuss how to end procrastination, let's first talk about how to recognize some critical warning signs which indicate that procrastination is getting out of hand.

Procrastination is the bad habit of putting off until the day after tomorrow what should have been done the day before yesterday.
Napoleon Hill

Chapter 2:

Learn To Recognize The 10 Warning Signs Of Procrastination

There are very many warning signs that indicate whether or not someone is a chronic procrastinator. Even though we cannot list them all, we shall look at a few that will serve as a guide to help you learn when your procrastination exceeds the norm.

#1 Avoidance and lack of commitment

Do you consistently put off activities that you want to accomplish? It does not matter what kind of activities they are; you could be putting off reading a book, starting an exercise program or starting drama classes. This is a telltale sign that you are procrastinating. Putting off things that you know you can accomplish today is a sign that you are not committed enough and are simply avoiding.

#2 Poor time management

Even though earlier we had indicated that procrastination is not a time management problem, it is possible that procrastination is the reason why you are always struggling to keep up with your daily meeting schedule. For instance, if you are always looking for an extension on projects that you are in charge of, you should start considering yourself as a chronic procrastinator.

#3 Perfectionism

Perfectionism could also be an indicator of procrastinative tendencies. Many are the times that you start something but obsess yourself about the idea that you should either do it perfectly right or do nothing instead.

With that mindset, you will find yourself stopping what you were doing because you are too obsessed about being perfect. If you start a creative project only to abandon it half way to commence on another creative project, it could be an indicator that you are procrastinating and are not committed, which as we have seen is a procrastination warning sign.

#4 Fear of failure or success

If we use the example of a creative project, fear of failure or success could be the reason why you don't complete projects successfully. If you are the kind that is easily distracted by the probability of failure or success in whatever you do, you will probably lose focus on what you are actually supposed to be doing now, which means you won't have the zeal to start right away.

A classic example is a situation where you may have a goal to self-publish a book but because of the fear that the book may not impress your target readers, you always feel you should wait a little longer so that you can gather more ideas and just be more prepared.

In many instances, you will probably give an excuse that you don't have enough time to dedicate yourself towards writing the book.

#5 Unrealistic goals and delusion of success

It isn't unheard of for you to just live in a fantasy world where you picture yourself living a luxurious life even when really you don't have a plan on how you want to get there. In as much as you may want to use the law of attraction to vibrate the right energies to manifest whatever you want in life, it is important to be realistic with yourself.

If you are not doing something now to help you in your journey towards manifesting whatever you want, you are just procrastinating; trust me, you will have to get up one day and do something in order to manifest what you want.

Bragging how smart you are without actually doing something to show that you are smart, is a classic example that you are a chronic procrastinator.

#6 Lack of confidence, passion and energy

This is very common in work related environments. You may find that your energies and passion for a specific project have diminished just because the CEO or project manager has changed a few aspects of the project.

On the other hand, lack of confidence in your skills and failure to take charge or control could be a telltale sign that you are procrastinating. Don't give excuses that you are not sure about your ability to get something done when you could start now. In any case, life is all about learning. So give yourself a break, you can always try again if you don't get it right the first time.

#7 A constant need for approval

In a work setting, if you keep on asking other members of your team their opinions on your work, it is a clear indication that you are procrastinating or avoiding something else altogether. It could also be a delay tactic, which as we have seen, is also a sign of procrastination.

#8 Lack of concentration

Lack of concentration can be influenced by many factors. However, chronic procrastination is the ultimate explanation for many of these factors. Let's face it, if you are the kind of person who excuses himself or herself because you tend to get easily distracted by other activities, chances are that you are procrastinating.

Would you have such distractions if you were trying to beat a deadline?

If you find that you keep on checking your email inbox constantly even when you are not expecting a specific email, it could mean that you are avoiding something else such as work or that you have lost your concentration.

In that case, you will not do what you should be doing now because you simply cannot concentrate.

Procrastination is the thief of time. Edward Young

#9 Excuses

If you are consistently making excuses for your failures, you are procrastinating. Excuses do not necessarily have to be failure related. If you keep on finding reasons why you should not talk to the girl next door, or start a workout routine, you are a procrastinator.

If you simply cannot get things done today for this reason or another, you need to start finding a solution for your problem as opposed to trying to justify why you do things the way you do.

#10 You constantly think "if I could have started earlier, I would be better off"

To be honest, everyone thinks that he or she could be doing better off today if he or she could have started something earlier. Others never start at all because they just feel that now is not an ideal time because of this reason or another. In many occasions, you may start something with friends only to give up midway because you are "busy" with this and that.

For instance, many people want to start an online business to make passive income. They simply cannot get the spark to start today. Their colleagues who may start much later will probably start making a considerably good income online such that they end up quitting their day job. You will probably only regret that you could have continued with your quest because you could at least be making something for yourself as opposed to relying on a 9-5 salary.

Chapter 3:

How To Overcome Procrastination Once And For All

Now that we have looked at some of the ways that you can use to identify when you are procrastinating, let us look at some of the ways that can help you overcome procrastination once and for all.

Adhere to deadlines

Deadlines should be treated as challenges to help you rise to the occasion and prove that you are capable of overcoming procrastination. In a work setting, adhering to deadlines could earn you trust points with your superior officers, which can go a long way into ensuring that the management views you as someone that can be trusted to deliver. This will actually catapult you in your career.

Adhering to a deadline means that you might need to push yourself and that will help you remain focused. If you have set to do something at a certain time, make sure that you do that task promptly and keep in mind that there is time for everything.

Take responsibility

The truth is that whether you have grand long term plans or have short term goals that you want to achieve, you will not achieve anything until you take responsibility for your inaction or action. If you keep on putting off going for dance classes while you want to become a dancer, do not blame anyone else but yourself.

Taking responsibility will wake you up to the fact that the direction that your life takes is squarely in your own hands.

With that mindset, you will know that every minute you don't spend doing what you were supposed to be doing, means that you won't do something you were supposed to do in the future because you were trying to beat a deadline doing the right thing at the wrong time.

Start easy and slowly

If you have been procrastinating about writing a book or doing house chores, start with the easy chores and work your way towards the harder ones. I have found that once you get started, you get motivated to continue as you go along. In the case of a book writer, most writing teaching programs will tell you that you need to start writing so that the content can come to you as you write. This is true for almost every aspect of our lives.

Have you ever waited to do something thinking how hard it is, only to realize that it is simpler than you had imagined when you had not commenced? This false idea about facts is one of the reasons why most of us procrastinate. It is relatively easy to conquer when you start easy and slowly, working your way up. As the old saying goes, Rome wasn't built in a day (keep in mind that they were laying bricks every hour!).

Value the goal

Procrastinating especially in a work related project or goal mainly happens because we have lost sight of the initial goal. If you are having this problem, it is always good to remind yourself why the project or task was important to you in the first place. This will effectively reignite your passion and ensure that you are motivated enough to carry on. If you cannot find focus on why the goal was important, think of the implications of not attaining that goal promptly. As Tony Robbins teaches us, there are two driving forces that make people doing the things they do (pain and pleasure). So, either remind yourself the pleasure you will receive when you achieve your goal, or the pain you will experience if you don't.

Have a positive attitude

Having a positive attitude towards life is very important to help you stop procrastinating. When you procrastinate because you are stressed or overwhelmed, you can easily overcome this by simple methods such as meditation and having a positive outlook in life.

Such strategies can help you remain focused and not get distracted by whatever you may come across at different times.

Keep in mind that concentration is the key if you are to stop chronic procrastination. If you are the kind of person who gets bored easily, you may be having a bad attitude towards different aspects of life, which you need to deal with if you want to eventually end procrastination.

Stop over thinking

If you have a fabulous idea that you think will revolutionize the world but keep on tweaking it so as to perfect it, you are simply using your fear of failure or success to take over your life; that's why you are always procrastinating. You have to realize that nothing is perfect but continuous development is what is considered growth.

Over thinking is what is keeping you from launching that technological breakthrough for mankind. Do you know that the some of the world's most complex problems have simple answers?

Avoid giving excuses and simply launch whatever you want to launch; then you can worry about whatever needs to be tweaked.

Take the first step in faith. You don't have to see the whole staircase, just take the first step. Martin Luther King Jr

Start anywhere

It is obvious that most procrastinators have a problem with their desire to get everything right the first round. Although planning is surely important, do not overdo it. If you must complete a task, jump in, start anywhere and build up as you go along. This is very effective in all life settings. If you have been over planning on when, or how to do the house chores, simply jump in and start anywhere. You will find that it will become easier to accomplish the goal once you get started. It is also an effective way of boosting your morale and confidence in your skill set. You may want to get some inspiration from Michael Jordan's experience that you don't have to be perfect to make the best out of life.

I've missed more than 9000 shots in my career. I've lost almost 300 games. 26 times, I've been trusted to take the game winning shot and missed. I've failed over and over and over again in my life. And that is why I succeed. Michael Jordan

Break down tasks into smaller chunks

Some tasks in their entirety can seem impossible. However, the truth is, these tasks can be quite easy to accomplish if you break them down into smaller tasks. Think about it, if you want to write a 500 pages romance novel, you don't have to see the 500 pages that you have to do but about 2 pages that you need to do in a day. You will be amazed by how easy it would be to attain whatever goals you have unlike convincing yourself that you don't have time to do a 500 pages novel.

Likewise, think of how hard it can be to clean a messy house that you haven't washed thoroughly in months. However, the task can actually be quite easy if you say that you will quick clean the house on one day then do a deep clean the following day. With that mindset, you will probably have cleaned every part of the house in less than a month.

Take action

Remember that even the tiniest progress is success. Do not wait until you have money to pay for a gym membership so that you can work out.

Instead, start by going for a morning jog as you wait for the gym membership payment. Taking action is the simplest method by which you will be able to overcome procrastination and achieve the goals that you have set out for yourself.

More precisely, you should take some direct action

that will help you to attain your goals. The trick to this is making sure that the feeling of accomplishment that you hoped to experience in the future is pushed into the present.

Don't give excuses, just start!

Recognize the procrastinator within you

One of the reasons why procrastinators never change their habits is because they do not acknowledge that they are procrastinating.

Another example would be an alcoholic who has to take the first step and admit that they are indeed addicted to alcohol. To overcome procrastination, you also have to recognize that you are a procrastinator.

Once you recognize this, you shall be able to remove the mental blocks in your way. You have to recognize the *procrastinators' motto* that you use and make sure that you are aware of it every time you use it. This will help you overcome procrastination easily.

"No pressure"

Pushing yourself is advised, after all how can you know your limits if you do not push yourself. Nevertheless, it is important to note that placing too much pressure on oneself will lead to perfectionism tendency, which as we have seen is jet fuel to procrastination.

Do not over think projects, do not say "this project has to be the best; it has to impress every one" since these types of thoughts are anxiety and stress catalysts which might lead you to procrastinate. Allow yourself to be human; imperfection is part of who we are. Start with trial and error in every project that you undertake and refine your work as you go along.

Avoid the "should be" mentality

"I should be rich", "I should be a dancer", "I should workout", "I should blah, blah, blah".

The sentiment of should invokes a lot of blame and guilt. This is because when you make a comparison between what you are doing (no matter how boring it is) and what you should be doing, you are focusing on what "could" have been, rather than focusing on what currently is. This can cause you to have feelings of failure, regret and depression. Ultimately, you will give up trying before you can even begin.

You can beat this by focusing on the now and how you feel; think of how amazing you will feel when you take action towards accomplishing your goals as opposed to how the current situation isn't where you should be since as you already know, wishful thinking, blame and guilt won't magically transform your situation.

Make the task fun

Let's be honest, some tasks are incredibly monotonous. For instance, tasks such a cleaning your home can become mundane. To make them fun, you can crank up your favorite song on the stereo and use the vacuum cleaner as an imaginary microphone as you vacuum. This will add a bit of fun to the task of cleaning.

In a work setting, you might also experience feelings of resentment if the tasks that you are performing are mundane. The trick to overcoming this is to make sure that you take constant breaks between working. Breaks do not have to be long; you can take a 5-minute break every one or two hours. The funnier the task is, the less likely you will feel the need to push it to a later date, which means you will have less incidents of procrastinating.

Chapter 4:

How To Use Smart And Effective Goal Setting To Get Things Done Now

As we had seen earlier, one of the things that most procrastinators tend to do is set unrealistic goals or try to perfect every single task. In order to get started on kicking out procrastination, you have to make sure that you use the S.M.A.R.T goal setting method.

Smart stands for:

Specific

Measurable

Attainable

Realistic

Timely

We shall look at how to set S.M.A.R.T goals that will make you less likely to procrastinate, which means you will get things done when they are supposed to be done.

S: Specific

Most procrastinators are known to set goals that are not specific like "I want to be rich" and "I want to start working out". These are all examples of unspecific goals. A specific goal would be; "I want to work out three times a week" or "I want to be rich before I am 40". A specific goal has a higher chance of being accomplished than a general goal. A specific goal is imbedded into your consciousness. In order to set a specific goal you need to have these considerations in mind:

#1: *Why*

Why is it important that the goal be achieved in the specified time? What are the benefits that will come out of achieving that goal? In the example of a work out, you might define that it is important so you can lose weight or simply be healthier.

#2: *Who*

Who is involved in the achievement of this goal? This is also important; as it will help you liaise with anybody who might be involved in the achievement of the goal. If we were to take an example of a work project, defining who is involved will help you ensure that they are apprised of any new information on the project.

This will create a symbiotic relationship that can speed up the completion of the project.

#3: *Which*

This is where you identify the constraints and requirements that must be met in order for the goal to be achieved successfully. What are the conditions that must be met if the project is to be completed successfully?

#4: *When*

In this aspect, you have to give a period within which you want the task to be accomplished. This will help you adhere to the timeline that you have set out for yourself. In the example of working out, you can say, "I want to work out 3 times a week starting from next week for a period of 4 or 6 months."

#5: *What*

In this question, you should define what you want to achieve and in what timeframes. If we were to take the example of the workout again (most people procrastinate about working out a lot) you have to define why you want to work out, what do you want to achieve? Is it better health or is it weight loss?

This will help you greatly in coming up with an effective way of achieving your goals.

#6: *Where*

Although you may want to attain different goals, you have to know which route you should follow to attain your goals. For instance, how can you be rich without seeking for opportunities actively?

Saying that you will go out tomorrow won't bring riches today! Defining where the goal must be accomplished will help you move in that direction or at least put you in the path of the said goal.

When setting specific goals, it is advisable to start with short-term goals. You can start by setting a daily goal like surface cleaning the house, then move on to a weekly goal of deep cleaning the house at least once and then a monthly goal of for example repainting the house.

M: Measurable

Setting goals that you cannot measure progressively will make it easier for you to procrastinate. It is critical that you establish a measurement criterion for your goal progress.

For instance, if your specific goal is to lose weight by a specific time, you must track and measure the progress and impact that the goal has had in your life.

Measuring progress on tasks can help you stay on track and motivated, and at the same time, give you pleasure in staying on track.

In order to measure your progress, you must ask yourself questions like:

"How will I know that I have made progress?"
"How much will it take to know that progress has been achieved?"

For instance, in order to lose 1 pound per week, you must give your body about 3500 calories less than what it actually needs; either by working out and/or adjusting your diet. You can use this benchmark to set a short-term goal of giving your body 500 calories less every day, to lose 1 pound weekly or 4 pounds monthly.

Measuring your goals will help you recognize when you achieve them. The more measurable your goals are, the easier it will be for you to know when you are giving excuses for not attaining them. Measurability also makes it easy to stay focused since you know what is expected of you.

A: Attainable

Once you recognize which goals are important to you, you then start compiling ways that you can use to attain these goals. You develop the correct attitude, abilities, skills and capacity to attain them. This helps you to recognize opportunities that you were previously unaware of that are geared towards your goal achievement. Attaining a goal will require that you plan well and set a time frame that will allow you to take steps towards attaining the foresaid goal. The best way to do this is to make a dream/ goal board.

List down all the goals that you may want to achieve daily, and work towards achieving them. Once you are done with the daily goals, move on to the weekly goals and then the monthly goals, this will help you ensure that goals, which might have previously seemed far away get closer and more attainable. The more attainable your goals are, the higher the likelihood that you will actually do them without giving excuses (procrastinating).

R: Realistic

If you set unrealistic goals, you are bound to experience feelings of despair when you do not achieve them. The criteria for measuring which goals are realistic and which ones are not is entirely up to you. While it may be unrealistic for someone to have a goal of losing 2 pounds weekly, it may be a realistic goal to someone else. Challenging but attainable goals are easier to achieve as the motivation towards their achievement is higher compared to that of goals that seem simple and easy to attain. A realistic goal must be one that you are able and willing to work towards its achievement. No matter how high you set your goal, you must make sure that it is measurable, as this will be the main factor to determine if a goal is realistic or not.

T: Timely

We all procrastinate; the difference is how often we do it. To make sure that your procrastination does not interfere with your goals, you must have a timeframe for their completion. This is especially important for either short or long term goals.

Failure to have a sense of urgency towards goal completion makes it extremely hard for you to track your progress. When you have not set a timeline for your goal completion, you may find that instead of working towards your goal completion, you occupy your time with tasks that are not geared towards the achievement of this particular goal.

Chapter 5:

How To Increase Your Productivity Using The Pareto Principle

The Pareto principle (80-20 rule) was named after Vilfredo Pareto, an Italian economist. This rule states that for almost all events 80% of the effects come from 20% cause. It is a commonly used rule of thumb in business.

To understand this principle, let us look at a few speculative instances. You may find that 80% of your business comes from 20% of your clients and 80% of complaints come from 20% of customers etc. So, how do you use this principle to increase your productivity? Let us look at a few ways.

Focus

Since the rule states that 80% of the effect comes from 20% cause, you have to focus on those activities that are producing the most results in your life. If 80% of your business comes from 20% of your customers, it would do you some good to make sure that the 20% are well taken care of. Additionally, you probably make 80 percent of your income from 20 percent of the time you spend working!

For every day activities, the best way to do this is to recognize which times you are most productive and perform tasks geared towards your goal achievement in these times. This will ensure that in the most productive time, you are performing a task that will have a great effect on your goals. When it comes to achieving goals, it is advisable to focus them on the 20% of the time that you are most active and productive since this will help you focus on the things that matter. Focusing on what brings most productivity will ensure that you actually do not procrastinate on the most critical activities.

Prioritize

Since you are mostly active for about 20% of your daily time, I advise you to make the 20% time count by prioritizing and performing tasks that are important during that time. If 80% percent of your friends are not true friends, it would be better to concentrate on the 20% of your friends that are true friends. If you find that 80% of your life is filled up of tasks that do not help you achieve your goals, then you should concentrate on changing this percentage to 20% of tasks that can help you achieve the most productivity in your life or work setting. Prioritize and perform the high value activities that offer the best results. If you are most productive in the morning, it would be a good idea to prioritize the most critical business tasks to be done in the morning.

Time management

The Pareto principle if used correctly can help you increase your time management skills. If you concentrate on accomplishing hard to complete tasks during the times that you are most active, you can free up your time allowing you to do more in the course of the day.

Practice

If you examine most of the tasks that we carry out on a day-to-day basis, you shall find how you can apply this rule in making the most out of your life. If you spend 80% of your day being unproductive, concentrate on achieving a lot more during the 20% time that you are most active, since this will increase your productivity. The more you use this rule in your daily life, the more it will grow into a habit, which means you will procrastinate less frequently. In the end, our habits are eventually those who determine our future.

Motivation is what gets you started. Habit is what keeps you going. Jim Ryun

Chapter 6:

8 Power Habits To Get You Started - And Keep You Going

As I have already mentioned, practice plays an important role in determining whether you will end procrastination. With practice, you can build habits that will definitely help you to get things done when they have to be done. Let's discuss some powerful habits that will help you deal with your procrastination problem.

#1 Focus on the now

Focusing constantly on long term goals will make you lose faith in the short term goals that together combined will effectively achieve these long term goals. Completing a full home cleaning procedure might seem like a hard thing until you start cleaning room by room. If you are writing a book, focus on completing a chapter now and then another tomorrow and another the day after. Eventually, you shall have a full book when you combine the chapters. Developing a habit of living in the moment as opposed to living in the future will help you to do what has to be done now without worrying about the future.

#2 Use a task manager

This is very effective for people who are having trouble with time management and task management as well. Task manager software and applications will help you know when and where you are supposed to be, what you are supposed to be doing and the time you should complete such tasks. You can also use a physical day planner, agenda or even a whiteboard, in order to plan your daily/weekly/monthly activities. At first, it will seem hard but once you get into the habit of following a task manager, it shall eventually form into a habit that you can perform without the help of the task manager.

#3 Take responsibility

Nurturing the habit of taking responsibility will help you maintain the mindset that you are liable to what happens in your life. If there are goals that you have set a specific timeframe for achievement, do not blame someone else when you are unable to achieve them. This will push you to work towards achieving these goals. Just by knowing that in the end you can only blame yourself and not provide any excuses, you will develop a mindset of getting things done without giving excuses why you cannot do them now.

#4 Eliminate distractions

Most procrastinators find distractions everywhere. If you tell yourself that you shall clean the dishes after watching a movie or you shall get to the project as soon as you are done with checking your email, switch off the TV or the computer and get down to business. When you want to be productive and achieve something, get rid of all distractions and concentrate on the task at hand.

In a work setting, you can use productivity apps to nurture new habits since some of these have features for disabling email notifications, social media sites and other sites that can make you lose focus of what you have to do.

#5 Be proactive

You have to realize that the goals you have set will not happen automatically unless you take action. Being proactive includes taking responsibility for all outcomes. Nurturing the habit of being proactive is the recipe for keeping off procrastination because you know that both success and failure is ultimately in your own hands.

#6 Prioritize

Learning how to prioritize is a sure way of maximizing productivity. If you were a sales representative, what would you do first?

Answer calls from 20% of your clients or do in house photocopies?

Prioritizing depends on the tasks that you deem to be more important than others and then performing these tasks first before any other. You can use the Pareto principle discussed above to master the art of prioritizing.

#7 Stop thinking, start doing

Stop over thinking everything and start doing. This is the only sure way to stop procrastinating permanently. Stop thinking how wonderful the food will be after you prepare it, start preparing it right away. Stop thinking how great life will be when you are a millionaire and start working towards achieving that goal. The more you nurture the habit of getting things done as opposed to just thinking about them, the easier it becomes for you to keep off procrastination.

#8 Set goals, achieve them, set others

One thing that is synonymous with effective people is that once they set goals and achieve them, they set some more as they realize what they are capable of. Don't just settle for anything you achieve simply because it feels good.

On the contrary, you should always aim for better.

After all, that is what life is all about, growth and progress. If you are not growing, then you are simply dying. Think about it.

This universal truth applies in everything in nature. With that mindset, procrastination will not start creeping back into your life simply because you have attained certain goals.

Arriving at one goal is the starting point to another. John Dewey

Conclusion

Procrastination if not dealt promptly, can become a serious problem that will only hold you back in whatever you want to pursue in life. I hope you benefited from this book and I would like to challenge you to take the next step, apply what you have learned, put everything into action and change for the better.

I will be more than happy to learn how this book has helped you in some way. If you feel you have learned something or you think it offered you some value, please take a moment to leave an honest review on Amazon. It would help many future readers who will be forever grateful to you. As I will!

To Your Success,
Adam Richards

ALL RIGHTS RESERVED. No part of this publication may be reproduced or transmitted in any form whatsoever, electronic, or mechanical, including photocopying, recording, or by any informational storage or retrieval system without express written, dated and signed permission from the author.

DISCLAIMER AND/OR LEGAL NOTICES:
Every effort has been made to accurately represent this book and it's potential. Results vary with every individual, and your results may or may not be different from those depicted. No promises, guarantees or warranties, whether stated or implied, have been made that you will produce any specific result from this book. Your efforts are individual and unique, and may vary from those shown. Your success depends on your efforts, background and motivation.
The material in this publication is provided for educational and informational purposes. Use of the programs, advice, and information contained in this book is at the sole choice and risk of the reader.